STEM Superstars

Elon Musk

by Anita Nahta Amin

Norwood House Press

Cover: Elon Musk is involved with many exciting projects.

Norwood House Press

For information regarding Norwood House Press, please visit our website at: www.norwoodhousepress.com or call 866-565-2900.

PHOTO CREDITS: Cover: © Jae C. Hong/AP Images; © AleksandarNakic/iStockphoto, 9; © Aleksei Potov/Shutterstock Images, 17; © Damian Dovarganes/AP Images, 21; © Duane A. Laverty/Waco Tribune-Herald/AP Images, 13; © JasonDoiy/iStockphoto, 11; © MSFC/NASA, 14; © Nichola Groom/Reuters/Newscom, 18; © Refugio Ruiz/AP Images, 6; © Thegift777/iStockphoto, 5

Hardcover ISBN: 978-1-68450-837-2
Paperback ISBN: 978-1-68404-631-7

© 2021 by Norwood House Press.

All rights reserved.

No part of this book may be reproduced without written permission from the publisher.

Library of Congress Cataloging-in-Publication Data
Names: Amin, Anita Nahta, author.
Title: Elon Musk : inventor / by Anita Nahta Amin.
Description: Chicago : Norwood House Press, [2021] | Series: Stem superstars | Includes index. | Audience: Grades K-1
Identifiers: LCCN 2019053763 (print) | LCCN 2019053764 (ebook) | ISBN 9781684508372 (hardcover) | ISBN 9781684046317 (paperback) | ISBN 9781684046355 (ebook)
Subjects: LCSH: Musk, Elon. | Businesspeople--United States--Biography--Juvenile literature. | Businesspeople--South Africa--Biography--Juvenile literature. | Inventors--United States--Biography--Juvenile literature.
Classification: LCC HC102.5.M88 A45 2021 (print) | LCC HC102.5.M88 (ebook) | DDC 338.092 [B]--dc23
LC record available at https://lccn.loc.gov/2019053763
LC ebook record available at https://lccn.loc.gov/2019053764

328N—072020
Manufactured in the United States of America in North Mankato, Minnesota.

★ Table of Contents ★

Chapter 1
Early Life..4

Chapter 2
Computers...8

Chapter 3
Space...12

Chapter 4
Cars and More...................................... 16

Career Connections 22
Glossary 23
For More Information 23
Index 24
About the Author 24

Chapter 1

Early Life

Elon Musk was born in Pretoria, South Africa, in 1971. He was quiet and small for his age. Bullies often teased him. He had few friends. But he had many ideas.

⭐ Pretoria is one of the three capital cities of South Africa.

5

Musk has big dreams for space travel.

Did You Know?
Musk grew up with his brother, Kimbal, and his sister, Tosca.

Some of Musk's ideas came from reading books. He liked books about space and computers. He even built model rockets.

The heroes in his books helped people. Musk wanted to help the world too.

Chapter 2

Computers

Musk learned to **code**. He made computer games. Later, he moved to the United States. He wanted to start his own company.

His brother joined him in California. They started a company. It made **online** maps. The brothers were poor. They lived in their office.

⭐ **People use many code languages to tell computers what to do.**

9

Did You Know?
At age 12, Musk sold a computer game he had made for $500.

But the company did well. They sold it. Then they started an online bank. It became PayPal. PayPal lets users pay money online. They made a lot of money.

The main PayPal building is in San Jose, California.

Chapter 3

Space

Musk wants humans to reach Mars. He formed SpaceX. It makes rockets. The first three rocket launches failed. Would SpaceX end? The fourth try worked! The rocket launched into space.

⭐ **Musk presents the SpaceX Dragon rocket. It is designed to take people and cargo into space.**

13

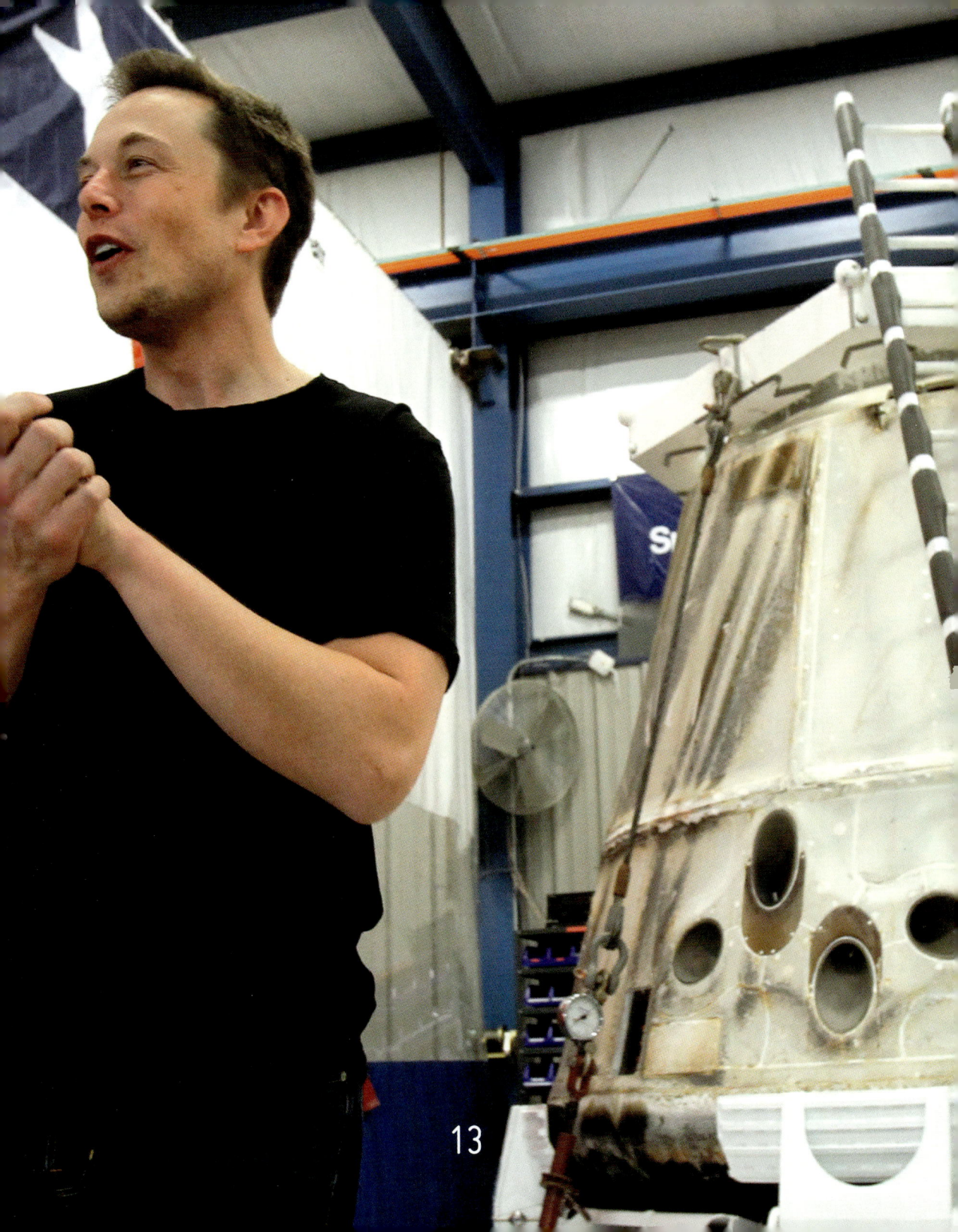

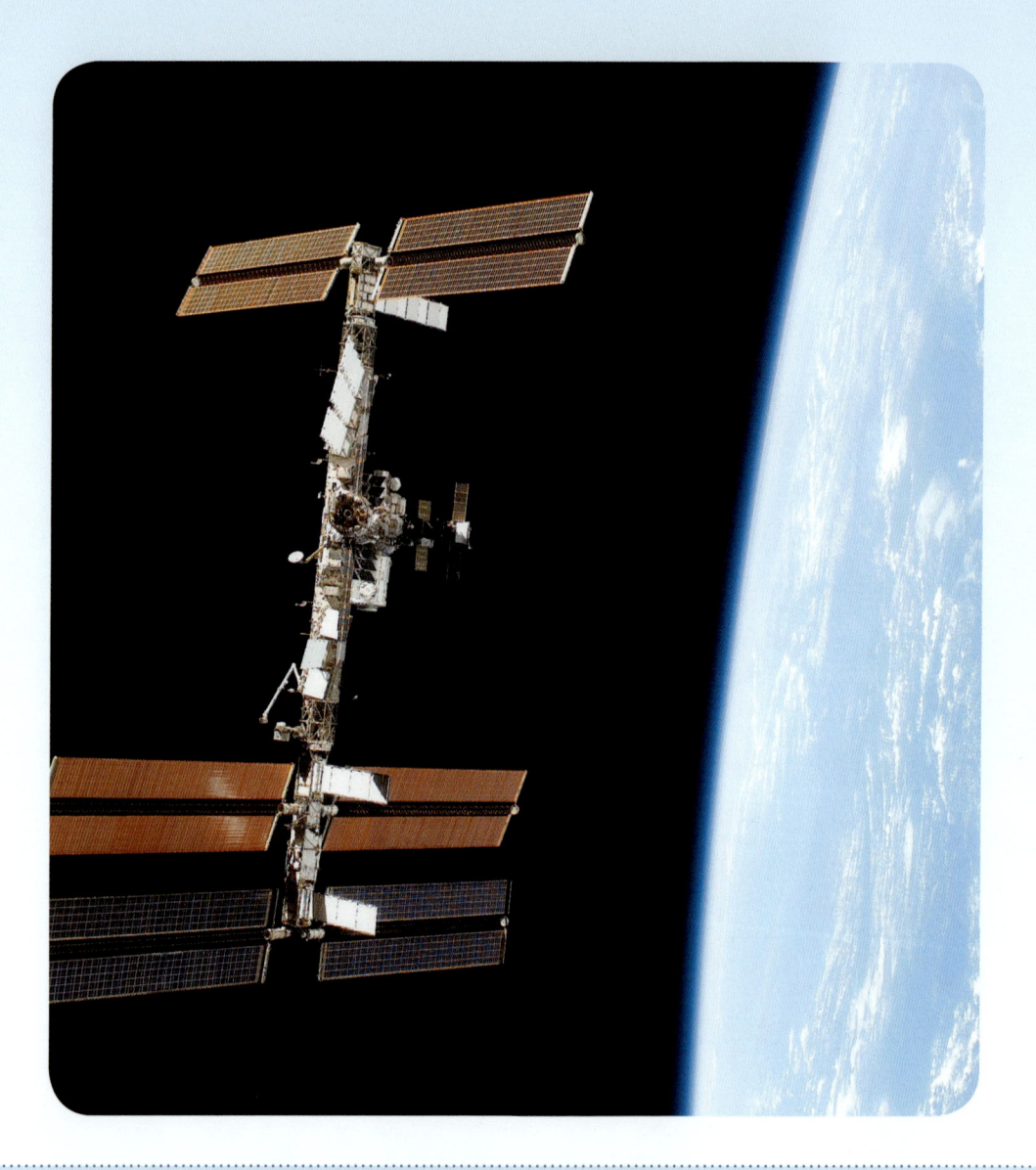

The International Space Station circles Earth. Astronauts living there study space and do science experiments.

Did You Know?
SpaceX's goal is to move people to Mars and the moon.

Musk's rockets now go to the **space station**. SpaceX takes supplies there. The rocket flies many trips. Old rockets could only launch once.

Chapter 4

Cars and More

Musk helped start the company Tesla. It makes cars. They use batteries. There is no smoke. The air stays clean. Tesla's goal is to make cars that drive themselves!

⭐ **Drivers plug in Tesla cars to recharge when they need power.**

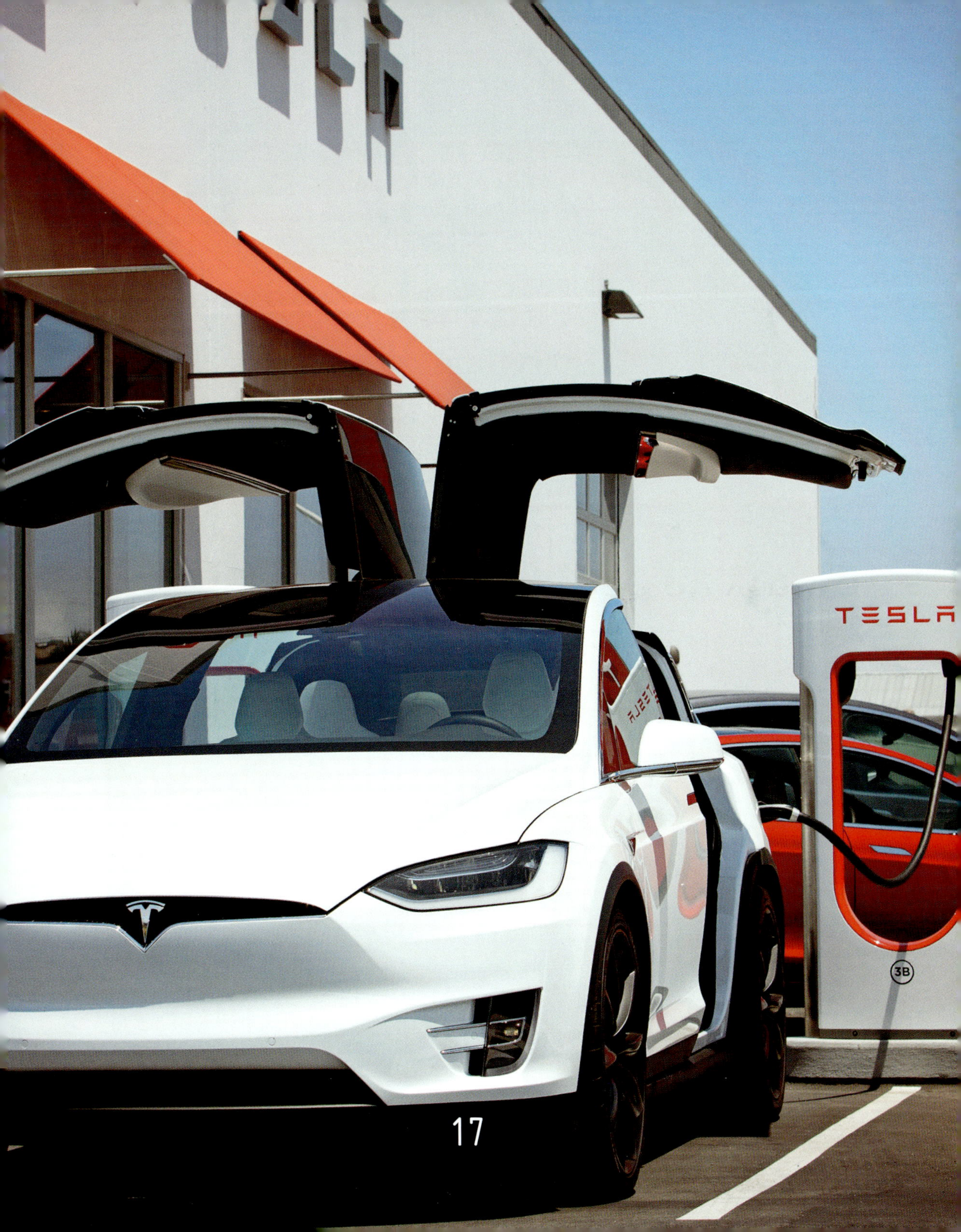
TESLA
3B

Tesla makes solar panels that look like a regular roof.

Did You Know?
Musk sent his car to space. It now circles the sun.

Musk has more ideas. He wants to make computers that read minds. He wants homes and cars to use the sun's power. He wants to build tunnels to make less car traffic.

Musk changed how people shop online. He changed how cars run. And he changed how rockets fly. He wants to keep changing the world.

Musk wants his ideas to keep helping others.

21

★ Career Connections ★

1. Elon Musk read many kinds of books. Go to the library or bookstore. Pick out a book and read it. Did you learn something new? How can you use what you learned?

2. Join a science club. Many schools have clubs for kids. So do libraries. Ask an adult to help you look for clubs.

3. Plan safe science projects at home. Ask an adult for help. You might find projects in books or online. Many stores sell science kits too. Or think of your own project.

4. Musk works with teams. Teamwork built cars. Teamwork built rockets. Join a sports team. Start a club. Pick some friends and work on a project together.

★ Glossary ★

code (KODE): To write instructions that tell a computer, phone, or app what to do.

online (ON-line): Connected to the internet.

space station (SPAYS STAY-shun): A spaceship where astronauts can live and that they use as a lab for research.

★ For More Information ★

Books

Janet Slingerland. *Coding 1, 2, 3*. Vero Beach, FL: Rourke Educational Media, 2019. This book introduces readers to computers and computer code.

Martha E. H. Rustad. *Space Travel*. North Mankato, MN: Capstone Press, 2018. This book shows what it's like to fly in a rocket into space.

Websites

Climate Kids
(https://climatekids.nasa.gov/fossil-fuels-coal/) NASA explains fossil fuel, solar power, and climate change.

Code.org
(https://code.org/student/elementary) Kids get hands-on experience with the basics of what computer code does.

NASA Kids' Club
(https://www.nasa.gov/kidsclub/index.html) This website teaches kids about space and NASA.

★ Index ★

C
Cars, 16, 19–20
Code, 8
Companies, 8, 10, 16
Computers, 7–8, 10, 19

O
Online, 8, 10, 20

P
PayPal, 10
Pretoria, South Africa, 4

R
Rockets, 7, 12, 15, 20

S
SpaceX, 12, 15

T
Tesla, 16

★ About the Author ★

Anita Nahta Amin is an Indian American author of children's fiction and nonfiction books. Many of her stories also appear in children's magazines and educational resources. She has degrees in biomedical engineering, electrical engineering, and computer engineering. A former information technology manager and business consultant, she now enjoys writing about STEM topics for children. She lives in Florida with her husband and twin children. She and her family hope to one day visit Mars.